Plc

Rod Campbell

The snake saw a dog.

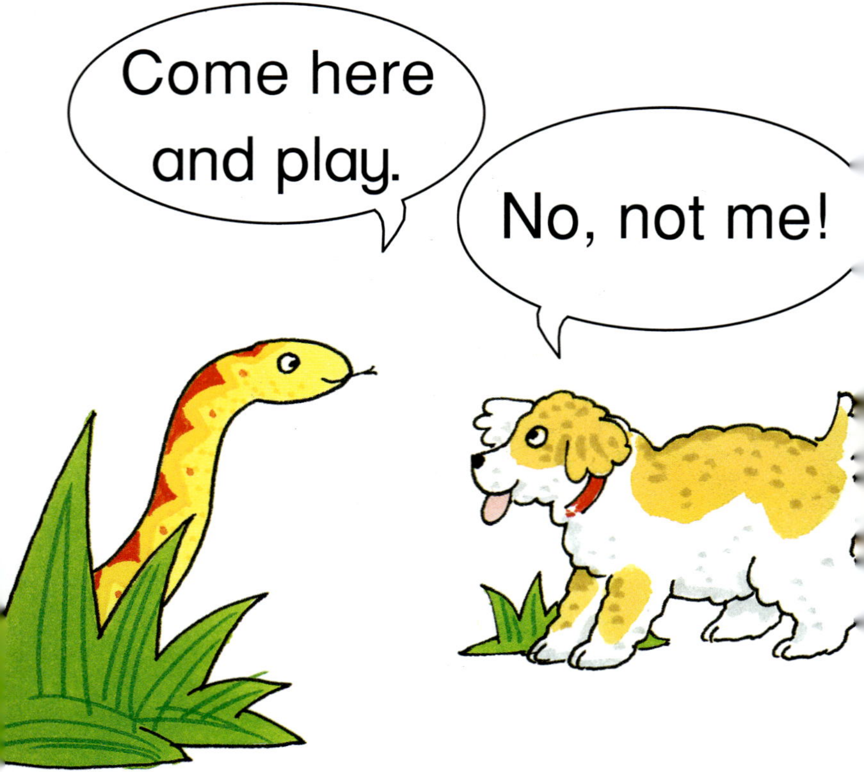
Come here
and play.
No, not me!

The snake saw a bird.

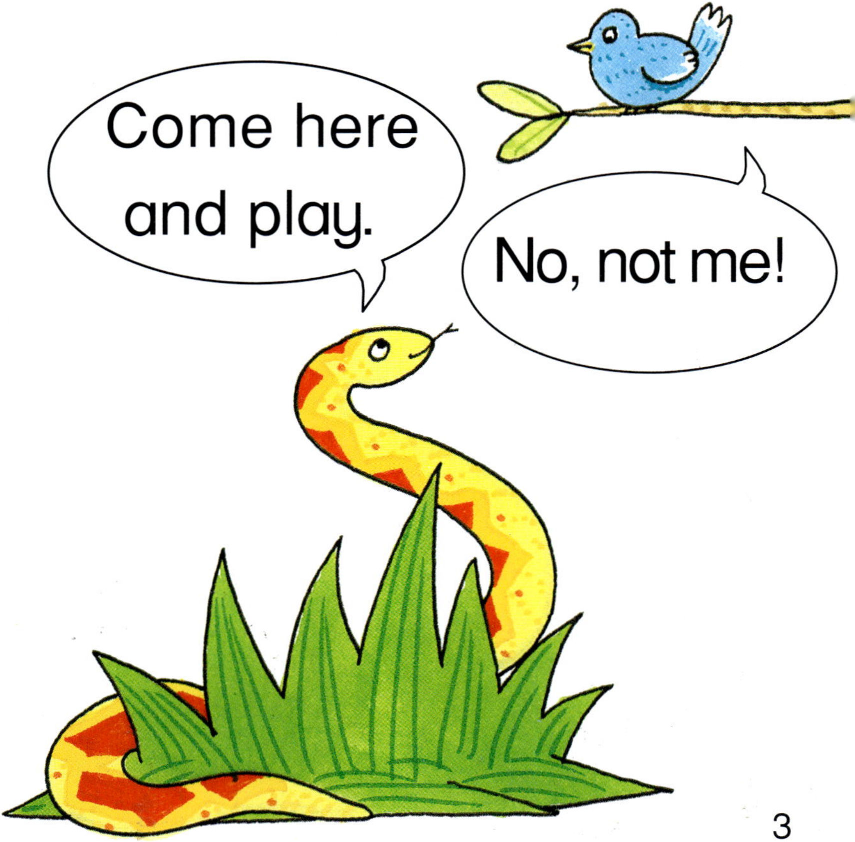
Come here
and play.
No, not me!

The snake saw a frog.

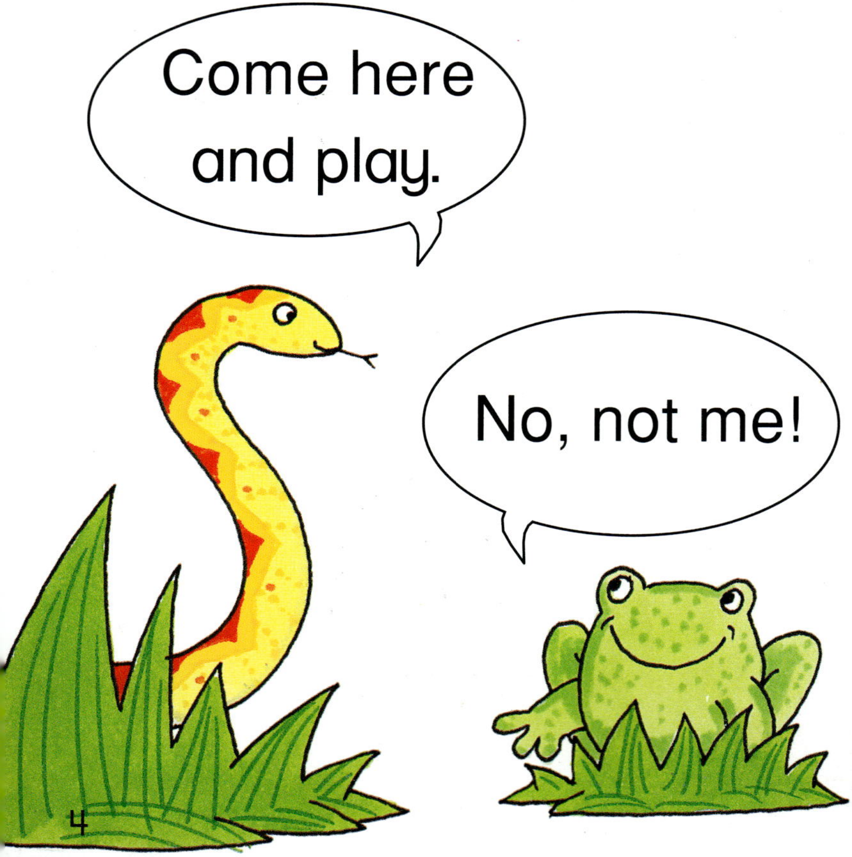
Come here and play.
No, not me!

The snake saw a rabbit.

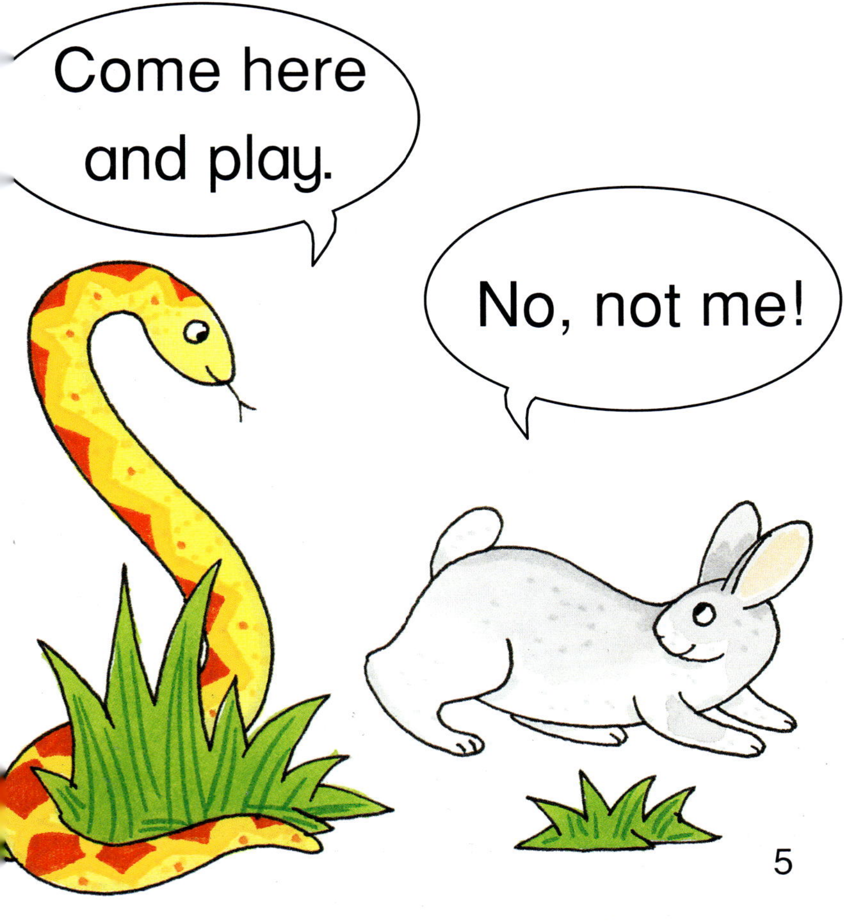
Come here and play.
No, not me!

Then the yellow snake saw a green snake.

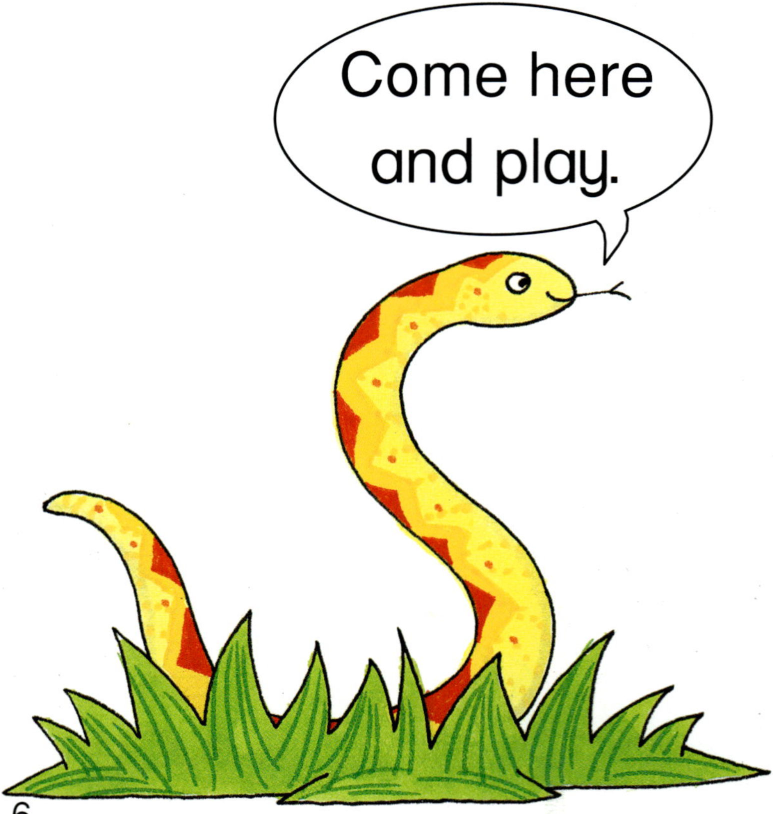
Come here and play.

Me?
Yes, I'll play!

And they played all day!